PASTORAL SUITE

ALSO BY JOHN MURO

In the Lilac Hour

PASTORAL SUITE

Poems by

John Muro

Antrim House
Bloomfield, Connecticut

Library of Congress Control Number: 2022909385

ISBN: 979-8-9855621-1-8

First Edition, 2022

Printed & bound by Ingram Content Group

Book design by Rennie McQuilkin

Front cover artwork "Prayer Flags in the Garden"
by Babette Barton

Antrim House
860.519.1804
AntrimHouseBooks@gmail.com
www.AntrimHouseBooks.com
400 Seabury Dr., #5196, Bloomfield, CT 06002

*This book is dedicated to Rennie McQuilkin,
publisher, editor, mentor and friend.*

ACKNOWLEDGMENTS

Grateful acknowledgement to the editors and staff of the following
 literary anthologies and journals in which these poems first appeared,
sometimes in slightly modified versions:

Across the Margin: "Dear Denise," "Summer at the Quarry, "Vertigo"
Amarillo Bay: "Adrift," "To My Grandchildren"
Amethyst Review: "Saint Boniface," "Plainsong," "Inversion," "April Morning"
Ancient Paths: "Oriole"
Ariel Chart: "For Linda," "In March," "Itinerants," "Swan of Tuonela,"
"Twilight, New Haven"
Aromatica Poetica: "Harboring Hyacinths," "Refuge," "Wild Privet"
Barnstorm: "Awaiting Autumn"
Bibliotheca Alexandrina: "Lethe," "Prometheus," "Whither Atlas?"
BlueHouse: "Breakwater"
Blue Heron: "Sycamores"
Blue Muse: "Aqua Corpus"
Clementine Unbound: "Aubade," "Befitting Blue," "Birch Mountain"
Ekphrastic: "Il Poeta"
Eunoia: "As Yet Undiagnosed," "Autumn Birches," "Common Tern," "False
Brooding," "Peacock"
Euphony: "Bird's Nest"
Eye to the Telescope: "Aegean Pools"
Foxglove: "Song," "Starlings," "Swallows"
French Literary Review: "Chagall's Still Life with Flowers," "The Boulevard
Montmartre at Night"
Freshwater: "Bird's Eye," "Egret," "Homestead," "Preserved"
Green Silk: "November"
Grey Sparrow Journal: "Angling"
High Window: "Afternoon at the Atheneum," "For Bobby," "Sisters," "Soapstone"
Hyacinth: "Arrival," "Hyacinths," "Sweetgale," "Water Gardens"
In Parentheses: "Au Printemps," "Green Turtle"
Literary Yard: "Deliverance," "Mid-Winter Night"

Mobius: "Evening in the ER"

MockingOwl Roost: "Another Life," "At Daybreak," "Cormorant," "I Wandered Early in My Sleep," "Near Uncas Point"

MORIA: "Cape Porpoise"

New England Poetry Journal/From the Heart: "Approaching Dusk"

Muddy River: "Flotsam," "Mid-November"

Neologism Poetry: "Loon"

New Square: "Promises"

OpenDoor: "For Anna," "In Late September," "Near Woodstock (VT)"

Orchards: "After a Storm"

pacificReview: "Hemlock"

Paddler Press: "Approaching Arcadia," "Elegia," "Notturno"

Penumbra: "Tiny Mercies"

Pegasus – Kentucky State Poetry Society: "Buckeye Tree," "Horseshoe Crab"

Poetica: "Day in Mid-October," "Milk Moon," "Ociosidad"

River Heron: "Peonies"

Sein und Werden: "Neon Pegasus"

Sheepshead: "La Passeggiata"

Sparks of Calliope: "Apparition," "Detachment," "Peregrine," "Vultures"

Sky Island: "After the Death of a Friend," "Cephaolopod," "Woodwinds"

[sub]liminal: "Vestige"

Third Wednesday: "Away from Water," "Daybreak," "Splinter"

Trouvaille Review: "In Spring, "Near Positano," "Nuit Blanche," "Winter Light"

Vita Brevis: "Morning, Berkshires," "White Tail"

WestWard: "Chalk"

Willawaw: "Moonlight," "Walk in October"

Writer Shed Stories: "Great Blue"

"In March" and "Aegean Pools" were nominated for a 2021 Pushcart Prize.

Special thanks to family and friends who have been a source of encouragement and inspiration during this exhilarating journey. I am most grateful for your ongoing support. In addition, heartfelt thanks to Kelli Russell Agodon, Babette Barton, Robert Cording and Rennie McQuilkin for their gracious support and contributions.

TABLE OF CONTENTS

I. Le Stagioni e il Mare (The Seasons and the Sea)

Aubade / 5
Water Gardens / 6
La Passeggiata / 7
Opaque / 8
Breakwater / 9
Adrift / 10
Daybreak / 11
Morning, Berkshires / 12
Flotsam / 13
Solstice /14
Aqua Corpus / 15
Winter Light / 16
Preserved / 17
Walk in Early Winter / 18
Mid-Winter Night / 19
In March / 20
Arrival / 21
Au Printemps / 22
April Morning / 23
In Spring / 24
Epithalamion / 25
Milk Moon / 26
Approaching Arcadia / 27
Deliverance / 28
Notturno / 29
I Wandered Early in My Sleep / 30
After a Storm / 31
Lives Once Lived in Flow / 32
Awaiting Autumn / 33
Cape Porpoise / 34

Summer at the Quarry / 35
Tidal Elegy / 36
Plainsong / 37
Inversion / 38
Aegean Pools / 39
Away from Water / 40
Seascape / 42
Moonlight / 43
Promises / 44
Autunno / 45
Itinerants / 46
In Late September / 47
Near Woodstock (VT) / 48
Migration / 49
Apparition / 50
Autumn Birches / 51
Walk in October / 52
Refuge / 53
Near Uncas Point / 54
Day in Mid-October / 55
Nuit Blanche / 56
Early November / 57
Mid-November / 58
Winter Birches / 59

II. Flora e Fauna (Flora and Fauna)

Great Blue / 63
Cephalopod / 64
Hyacinths / 66
Preservation / 67
Peacock / 68
Spider Flower / 60
False Brooding / 70

Vultures / 71
Mountain Laurel / 72
Bird's Nest / 73
Loon / 74
Wild Privet / 75
Vespers / 76
Green Turtle / 77
Colibri / 78
Sycamores / 79
White Tail / 80
Cormorant / 81
Harboring Hyacinths / 83
Egret / 84
Oriole / 85
Sweetgale / 86
Horseshoe Crab / 87
Common Tern / 88
Peonies / 89
Lodge with Pond / 90
Peregrine / 91
Sloths / 92
Swallows / 94
Buckeye Tree / 96
Starlings / 97

III. Cuore e Casa (Heart and Home)

Angling / 101
After the Death of a Friend / 102
Woodwinds / 103
Another Life / 104
Song / 105
Near Positano / 106
As Yet, Undiagnosed / 108

Befitting Blue / 109

Woodlake / 110

Detachment / 111

Chalk / 112

Effects / 113

Homestead / 114

Soapstone / 115

The Sisters / 116

Il Poeta / 117

The Peabody Museum, 1965 / 119

Whither Atlas? / 121

Saint Boniface / 122

For Anna / 123

Dear Denise / 124

Afternoon at the Atheneum / 125

Travelogues at the Bushnell Memorial / 126

Birch Mountain / 127

For Bobby / 128

At Daybreak / 129

Bird's Eye / 130

Valle de Mulini / 131

For Linda / 132

Splinter / 133

Vestige / 135

Prometheus / 137

Hemlock / 138

Chagall's *Still Life with Flowers* / 140

The Boulevard Montmartre at Night / 141

Elegia / 142

Neon Pegasus / 144

Vertigo / 145

Evening in the ER / 146

Tiny Mercies / 147

Ociosidad / 148

Swan of Tuonela / 149
Tetterboard / 150
Homebound / 151
With Affection, Athens / 152
Twilight, New Haven / 153
Lethe / 154
To My Grandchildren / 155

About the Author / 159
About the Book / 160

*Poetry should surprise by a fine excess . . .
and appear almost a remembrance.*

               – John Keats

PASTORAL SUITE

I. LE STAGIONI E IL MARE (The Seasons and the Sea)

Aubade

I wake to sleep, and take my waking slow. – *Roethke*

Early Sunday morning ambling in awe beneath
the dense canopies of trees, their scarlet
satchels slung across the rounded shoulders
of boughs and dangling like the languid arms
of neighbors still loafing abed. Now a starless
silence gives way to the hiss of sprinklers popping
up their tiny, saw-toothed heads, dispensing looping
sprays of water like a benediction; the rhythmic
repetition of plumes in precise industry splintering
into prisms of light, a carousel of mists and arcing
streams as the metallic rustle slows and abandons ear,
giving way to the sweet happenstance of birdsong,
the brittle scuttling of fallen leaves and slack channels
of blue unspooling among mottled river stones of cloud.

Water Gardens

Far end of summer and evening comes
with stars as soft as swans,
medieval gold floods across the lawn,
a distant thunder drums

from somewhere moon-distant, beyond
the tree-line, and a lithesome
wind brushes across the open mouths
of blossoms in a paddle-hushed sound.

Dew-dripping grass and a horizon of plum,
near-glimmering, appear years from dawn
or winter's blue, enfeebled tongue's
monastic requiem.

Gardens of snowdrift and pearled abalone
rise, flowers flourish in sponge-soft stone.

La Passeggiata

Daylight drawing down
and a meager light lingers
enticing the curious
out into a confluence
of sun and shadow –
older men inclined
to reverie humming
to themselves and
women moving from
behind the solitude
of windows licked
by early evening sun
to take in the recurring
dream that forms near
dusk when summer air
cools and bestows a
blessing to each sense:
the sputtering gurgle
of fountains; the scent
of cypress, cedar and
thyme; the faint song
of a wingless thrush;
and the late spooling
of clouds slowly
giving way to the
purpling of air and
bronze rivets of stars
boarding up the sky.

Opaque

Fog sets out
in slippered feet,
sleepwalker slow,
and with hands
released from ice
pushes away from
up-right stones, smoothing
the day's rough textures
of porous rock and
brittle reeds before
feathering the edge of
conifers. Now landlocked,
it drifts down to finish
its final tasks: latching
attic windows, stacking
firewood and staining
the splintered garden
gate before dutifully
shaking out the bed-
sheets, folding the last
of the laundry, and
then settling, heart-
sick and apron-poor,
upon the porch,
trying to recall the
time of day, the
season and what else
remains to be done.

Breakwater

Perched upon a plinth of rock, decades old,
crafted from a mixture of mortar and stone,
craters and cavities, hollowed just below
the waterline, form a brittle honeycomb,
which tongues of salt have exposed

in the going out of tides. Designed
to separate earth from water,
it's a barrier near free-fall, inclined
to lean hard into sun, eastward,
its structural integrity undermined

and no longer plumb. It is pressed
from behind by earth and gravity,
a constant, irrepressible caress,
subverting with stealth, relieving
the structure of heft and ballast.

Opposing forces work in cruel device
to crater, topple and eventually swallow
and return wall to water. So it is with a life
tending to a state of perpetual repair, knowing
it will end in a loose uprooting and indifference.

Adrift

Twilight's turning out the daytime sky as if
it were a pilot light, blue flame fluttering into
vapor, leaving the edges of heaven fringed
in rippled scatter. Shadows lengthening as
the last play of light is pulled down to water.
Overhead, the hushed, dust-soft sweep of bats,
the slow, easy lilt of wind dawdling in languor,
and stars sinking between clouds in bright idleness.
Leaf-burdened branches catch and then release a cold,
celibate moon into apertures of orange-yellow light.
And I see how this may well be the way life abandons
us at some near-distant, mystical hour. Luminous
in parting, it too becomes a thing unburdened and,
set adrift, brightly burns as it spins away from us.

Daybreak

Holding close to the water-
line on a day when nothing
rises, a sky hewn from dusk
has been pressed towards
earth like slabs of granite
bound with mortar made
from soot and ash. Between
the far horizons, thunder-
heads, barrel-vaulted,
hang in tight-fisted swirls
mottled with dollops of ether,
forming a canopy the color
of basalt and brackish water,
and the only other inhabitant
is a solitary, sick-for-blue
gull – plummeting from
heaven without the means
of ascent, tangled in the
splintered threads of gill-
nets thrust towards shore
by the morning tide.

Morning, Berkshires

This day tests the value
of vision, all distance
measured by ear: the
emerging particulars
of acorns, in hushed
hurl, slapping the under-
side of leaves and plucking
ground; of lake waters
lapping in muffled slush
beneath a ridge line half-
hidden in mists.
A catbird's cry, fraught with
anguish, moves against me
and gives voice to a fore-
boding that settles uneasily
after an evening interspersed
with rain. Then this strange
and shapeless silence and
an emptiness that seems
unfathomable – feeling
more than a day's dying
and wondering what it is
that we are married to, what
has changed and what, more
precisely, has been taken from us?

Flotsam

The truth is I heard little of what
you said that night beyond *lost*
and *forgotten* since I was listening
to my own particular grief and
the slush of tides settling into
refrains of ruffled erosion, noting
how each wave silently advanced
and loosely cradled slivers of light
just before breaking apart, or taking in
the night sky, worn smooth as
river stone, with its delicate
collection of stars adrift in cold
isolation and a soon-upon-us moon
that looked like a road-side flare
I thought to borrow, thinking it
might lead me away from those
questions I dared not answer,
knowing each word between us
could be a misstep and our final
moments would be spent parsing
words or reconstructing phrases,
yet never realizing how it might
also illuminate the way the waves
constantly drifted in and out of
themselves or the cloudy wreckage
that had been hopelessly set adrift
and was slowly floating away.

Solstice

A winter day near ending
and dusk has been spread
across the sky like a coat
of horsehair plaster,
feathered eastward into
finely troweled vapor,
glazing leafless boughs
and snow-hushed groves,
blurring bodies of still
water with a citrus splatter
while snow, in spirals of
tasseled foil, rises like
turnbuckles affixing a
frozen earth to heaven,
leaving a chasm where,
on this shortest of days,
hope and dusk's faraway
ashes are swept and then
blown, like trembling stars,
into an abundant mass of
darkness that's hard pressing,
in selfsame sprawl, against us.

Aqua Corpus

Air's frosted and silvered by salt and the winter
sky's so impossibly blue one could be forgiven
for thinking all that was once known has
been forgotten and these mottled branches
of sycamore have been transformed into
gnarled colonies of coral and clusters of
desolate seabed; nearby husks of hydrangeas
and winterberry may as well be sponges nudged
towards a waterline by some wayward current
while low clouds gather like schools of guileless
tangs and damsel fish to survey the dull chrome
spatter of a green-house – a caravel somehow
battered and brushed ashore, the expanse
of sail lifting feebly like a wing that's torn
or tearing in a tangle of wind, though we,
too, are wind-tossed and in bitter need
of ballast – disoriented castaways stranded
amid iridescent tides while the elements
conspire to transform the shoreline into
something utterly strange and not of this world.

Winter Light

On a day fashioned by cold and mid-winter sun,
the estuary unfolds like an esplanade in pale,
pleasing light, bordered by the glazed stalks of
marsh grasses, leafless trees and small knolls
of overturned boats, the still water collecting
colors that spread out on a thin film of ice
like a second skin. Arabesques of snow take
to air in an intermittent winter wind,
glistening in the loose apparel of pearl with
tinsel trim, drifting down towards shallows
where round tidal stones sparkle
like shell casings. Day deepening, we see how
all things are buttered by day's after-light,
and how, like a soul, it diffuses into – and
yet draws apart from – all things and how,
even at night, when all the world's asleep,
it can still break upon the world and curve
back upon itself so that all things appear
upside down with stars winking as if they
were shattered shells, lavish ornaments or
flecks of gold glistening in currents of clear water.

Preserved

An ornate necklace adorns the lake,
its combed strands of pearled white
advancing earth, though the center
pulp softly churns. The ice makes
for a half-healed and lightless
surface. The cold reassures;
an after-life gray will overtake
the lake's receding brightness
and still the far interior.

Random, pendant flakes
drift in tangled flight;
they rise, fall, linger
and seem to congregate
like moths in mid-air despite
a sudden down-rush
of wind. All's in a state
of snow-bright darkness
never knowing, for sure,
if light's a thing let in or out.

Walk in Early Winter

A sun too distant
and a forbidding wind,
snow flakes exploding
amid shards of ice;

a morning walk
aborted, and then
his silent goading;
I think twice

but continue on
farther than intended,
though steps are slowed
by drifts of snow and ice.

Each leaf's still radiant,
folly gold and red.
Our path home
is longer and less precise.

Mid-Winter Night

i

The moon, wandering low
and motherless,
a misbegotten element drifting
in and out of sight –

as if its silent tide of light
were too heavy to lift
from this world of snow
that's eerily winter-hushed.

ii

Flourish of clouds slowly close
and extinguish what little light
gravity has left:
all's winter-dark and emptiness.

Darker marvels all about us:
jeweled ice and cloudbursts of breath;
shards of snow in tempered flight,
and a cold only the dying know.

In March

It is the pause that comes between
the seasons breathing in and out,
hillsides neither white nor green:
a landscape that's note-
worthy for its rampant emptiness.

Clouds of coal-dust in gritty sheen
curl tight as wood-knots;
the deeper silence of leafless trees
with baffled boughs
beneath a sky forever bleak and sunless.

The damp fragrance of fields, thinned
by frost. Caught in the throat
of a small bird – a winter wren
perhaps – an expiring note
that drifts to whisper or something less.

Holding out for the sequin-
bright air, moon-burst fraught,
when life wells up from these rutted fields and trees
in hungry thrust, turning from what is now
but a world of damp and dreary idleness.

Arrival

March is leaning hard
into April, though one
can sense the world's
softening and pressing
on towards the grandeur
of green. Woodlands are
now wind-spun and drink
in the day's darkness, and
streams are swollen with
snow melt and stirred to
motion by knurls of ice
swept into a confluence
of upland scrim and water,
and even though the boughs
still bear more sun than
leaf, all appears near-
abundant: birds from
away are soon arriving
like wishes finally granted,
and crocuses purple the
earth like paper-weights
holding fast to smaller
pockets of land, while
a flourish of forsythia,
straw-spun yellow, hides
tendrils of maidenhead
fern as they rush to prop
up this translucent bowl
of heaven over-flowing
with a winter's worth
of half-remembered blue.

Au Printemps

For Timothy Francis

I welcome it, those in-between hours
of late winter when daylight starts
lengthening and slowly turns from
darkness; the slow leave-taking of ice
without murmur into muddled pools;
the tremor of raw, gold-turning light
up and beyond winter-withered boughs;
and outcroppings of rock now rising
up thru frosted soil like small pods of
pilot whales; and everywhere the ground
appears milled by tides. Gray split fence-
posts dangle like splintered bones,
propping up the nascent froth of forsythia;
ruffled, wind-shorn nests of lichen
cup pale eggs, a garden gate
left askew gives way to alien artifacts,
and unbudded saplings push thru a
cold calm aching for light. Other things,
too, hobbled by weather and an obdurate
frost, are unthreading and newly exposed
like the long, thick knuckles of maples
jutting thru drifts of snow, each one
bearing witness to a season they're slowly
releasing and another they're lifting back to life.

April Morning

A pair of sparrows, shut-ins
buried in the lower boughs,
draw upwards in giddy banter
to unzipper this day, giving
rise to earth's slow yawn and
easeful stretch into a yellow
lather of light, while darkness
scurries beneath the sodden
stoops and sloped porches
of houses just come back to
life. The last vestiges of a
moonless night have been
folded and tucked into the
inky wounds that sit between
the branches of conifers as
a drowsy wind, frost-chilled,
meanders across an expanding
pasture of sky before its fateful
stumble, spilling from its heavy,
ice-laden bucket more blue than
this day can possibly bear.

In Spring

Winter's teetering and
certain to fall, with sap
rising in wooding hills,
new-leaf-pungent, silted
trails in mud-thick thaw,
and everywhere buds of
hardwood ooze scarlet
and wisps of smoke, like
lassos, spool back and
harden into burl knots
of blue while the soft
percussions of bird song
continue to hurt hearts
and confound ears. Closer
in, the doleful thud of
hooves, the soft stutter
of loose gravel and breaths
taken by a shambling wind
burdened with scents of
freshly milled and mitered
cedar and musk of dung
wafting past as the silver
gristle of frosted mulch turns
back into a breezy blur
of grass and three-starred
trillium purples stream
banks and pasture and
all the world's at last
unspun from stupor,
and come back to life.

Epithalamion

On such a day why wouldn't I believe
a single breath created life? The wind,
a sweet confusion, lilac-pungent, cleaves
to me, and fields of wildflowers seem to
explode in loose assembly, giving up
form for color, exchanging odors and
mingling with the scents of meadow hay
and traces of cedar just released by ax;
insects pestering fields, birds releasing
morning from their throats, and wood-
lands redolent of dew, pine-swell, and
the woolly shoots of fern and wild berries
and a sudden want to ladder up into a
sky of delphinium blue while light hangs
in the air, never waning, filling every furrow
of freshly tilled earth and leaching down-
stream upon the surface of water, bronze-
gold gleaming, past the river bank holding
bright candles of birch, while garlands
festoon the church-yard and windows
of painted glass, praying for this day
to somehow linger and, with dumb luck,
find you still there calling me home.

Milk Moon

Eased from dusk,
a barge near toppling
is unberthed from the
horizon as if it were
laden with last of the
world's gold bullion,
dripping with light.
Oiled clouds parting
like unstitched veils,
as the moon forswears haste
and lifts, in slow splendor,
away from the edge of
earth into a pocket of
plush darkness, and all
things prone to wander –
birds, dreams and a
whimsical wind – pause
and loiter in eerie silence
and even the Herdsman
abandons his hunting
dogs before slowly
ambling in dim majesty
across the barrens of heaven.

Approaching Arcadia

Morning's blurred smooth by mists and
wind's snuffed out by the damp of autumn
air. Sun, still a brush-stroke of soluble
light and leaves once wedded to boughs
are now widowed as I sink into the soft
tangle of quickening-to-duff needles
discoloring the woodland floor
and ankles wade into an armada of fern,
serrated sails in green-bronze billow
adrift beneath the sweetly confusing
odor of pines that shadow a silent
stream framing the far edge of pasture.
Here, the blurred bliss of birds is
everywhere: the pump-handled tanager
hidden in high grass; clutch of bitter-
sweet – cinder of oriole glistening in nest –
or the thin, trailing branch of thrasher
foraging for food before the audible
slather of a gravelly road beyond the
matted contours of a soft and mossy earth
that swallow sound and the dim coin-glint
of images we would just as soon unsee.

Deliverance

Wind gusts, strong enough to lift small boats from
the surface of water, pelt piers and hasten
the undoing of long-leaning trees; shredding thick
hedgerows in such a way the lower leaves tangle
and spin like minnows in shallow water. Clouds
of galvanized gray churn as if thrown up from
the sludge of salt-marsh, and the whole shoreline's
lurching and being taken back to the sea floor. I turn into
the gale, forcing eyes and lips shut as I hear in the
distance a timber mast crack and the flailing wing-
beat of a crumpled canvas. With cold clarity, I lean
windward and offer up my simple gift of body, and now,
an orphan of want and need, I traverse the terrible emptiness
among stars glistening like opalescent scales of dismembered fish.

Notturno

As if it were feeling its way
across the harbor, fog clings
to the masts of boats for
ballast before making landfall,
its pale gold and onyx train
rippling like an underskirt
of silk, and its gross profusion
of fabric unfurling and then
refashioning both marsh and
meadow before coming to
rest upon the snowy terraces
of Queen Anne's Lace and
verandahs of Wooly Yarrow.
Well-bedded, it will disrobe,
whitening hollows, muffling
sounds and damping starless
air, before lifting its still-gloved
hands to extinguish the first
tortured light of morning sun.

I Wandered Early in My Sleep

I wandered early in my sleep,
laid demons out towards a restless sea:
the soft-shouldered rocking of nomadic tides
might ease this widowed grief.

Pallid light of stars kindles then leaps
from tattered waves to buoy,
muffled drum of bell, confused,
rises then dissolves into foam and reef.

Moonlight, half-drowned, spills deep
into chambers where refluent trees
and thread-like flowers drift then fuse
to coral's backbone of ruffled leaf;

their profound emptiness finds relief
in flickering currents spun from glass. Sea
kelp and sprays of knotted-wrack lie
tangled like serpents in pools of tidal drift.

After a Storm

Early morning light's pearl-lustered
and air takes on a liquid look. Back-
sliding channel is near-empty, mud-dry,
with just a thin trickle of stream,
like a muscle of eel, slithering between
the bent reeds and cattails once as high
as a house: a landscape that's been redacted
by the addition and subtraction of water.

How steadily the dead drifted down and tides
sought to draw them back to their beds,
released them to surface and deposited
them in this fetid cache of marooned gore.
The remaining water is a curiously cured
blend of linseed oil, kerosene and silt –
a color approaching stippled lead –
that's diluted and eerily guided

by wind towards a harbor that's tied
tight as a drum skin, its surface stretched
to near-translucence. Hard to reimagine waves
that surged like marauding legions in full
armor, rising in seething fury and toppling
in cataclysmic descent, exploding in such a way
landfall seemed unexpected. Now just the hushed
murmur and tambourine shudder of outgoing tides.

Lives Once Lived in Flow

Lives once lived in flow, in the spin-
drift of tides, are now eerie remnants
that have been carried, then left, to shore
in muted timbrel. The olio of phosphor-
escent scum moon-glistens in decay
and appears to frost a harlequin display
of bloated spiral wrack, eel grass
and lime-green fronds of Irish moss;
the past is present now and sun-washed;
heaps of contorted shells are bleached
milk-teeth white; and a near-rancid scent
forms a strange, uneasy covenant
with wind, as the odor grows more dense –
here, death comes clean and without pretense.

Awaiting Autumn

Even on the best of days, I confess
to a want to hurry summer towards
its end, and welcome the lessening
of sun and indolent mornings that
open into the luminous down of blue
afternoons, and take in the descent
of bereaving mists that drift over
hills of hard-woods thru gaunt groves
of birch and fern, then hauntingly
linger within a split-rail expanse
of pasture, and what little is left of
leaves hang like bandages clotted
by the dried blood of autumn.
But that season of grief and going
remains a life-time distant, tucked
beneath the crawl-spaces of these
encrusted cottages that are slowly
sinking into the strand, or loosely
cradled somewhere beyond the fetid
plunder of salt-marsh framed by the
sash of a double-hung window,
cracked glass adorned with chapped
paint and spittle, leaning away from
land, panes open to the undulations
of petitioning surf, gull-squabbling
skies and the ruffling of laundry
strung across yards like nautical
flags signaling our meek surrender.

Cape Porpoise

Skillet-black ooze and primal scum cling
to the ankles of gangly docks, and the pleats
of channels hold the still breath of decay
and deep-down things – shells, salt grasses,
bones and scales – the sweet, dank distillations
of days half-broken. The chirr of flies sings
oysters open; contrails spewed in a pungent
heap of onion-orange pulp and follicles
no longer flailing limply in cold currents;
rather, the foul fissures of a primeval earth
are exposed at low tide. Somewhere, scented
clusters of sea rose dissolve to fragrance
beneath swallows in buckshot shredding
air; and, from behind the gold patina of
candle lamps icing cottage windows,
sleepless souls take in the slurred diction
of tides and the glistening arc of sea-
spray, while linen sands, in a color that
most resembles liquid amber, shimmer
in warm winds that carry with them
the tender trespass of curious children.

Summer at the Quarry

The next best thing to love,
you insisted, wasn't the delicious
trespass or even the precipitous fall,
but leaving land wingless for some
point of near-distant air just
beyond the fingertips that gave
way to howls and the sudden,
panic-stricken plunge into a
shock of cold water leaving
one of us with a desperate need
for breath and a hunger for one
last chance to take in a summer
sky that had just transformed
into a fire as large as a county
with contrails of cloud expanding
like the luminous remnants
of some cosmic explosion that
delicately burnished brownstone
walls and spread across the water's
surface in an iridescent slick
of laurel-pink and purple oil,
and leaving me, in your view,
unable to distinguish the purely
pleasurable from the beautifully
tragic or reminding me of my
perverse want to favor the empty
allure of the ephemeral over the
cruel, reckless and desperate
beauty of the here and now.

Tidal Elegy

Between early morning and mid-day hours
I set out towards the marsh beyond hedges
of inkberry and the bay's broad mouth
where a putrid odor of decay rises and
stings every pore of my body. I take in
the jeweled gore and bric-a-brac of
bone and flesh in a millennium of muck:
earthly constellations of iridescent scales
and lime-white shells, and the carcass
of a gull, its body lodged in cruel
contortion with its sulfur-bright eye
gazing upwards as if blue was its first
and final hunger, body half-decayed
and encased in silted ribbons of marsh
as it too, slowly sinks into beds
of bottomless black. Patient in parting,
all manner of extremities are lodged in
a thick ooze and appear like things brought
out of, instead of returning, to earth.
I pick my way past a swarm of midges
singing through gnawed bones of fish,
jaws hinged open and entrails cleared,
still bubbling breaths of silver filament,
to see what else remains of this fetid feast
bleached by time and so rich with endings.
Throughout these shallows, earth has been
made easy by tides and the quartz-speckled
sediment that takes all things down towards
a dolorous death where voices rise up upon the wings
of monastic birds wheeling and slowly perishing into air.

Plainsong

"Bonum est diffusivum sui"
(The good pours itself out)
    – St. Thomas Aquinas

Mid-summer sky, hallelujah bright,
waves rising in exultation, gulls tilting
for ballast and slowly rising like a
devotion in gusts of salt-glazed air.
Wooden grids of cottage windows
are filling up with candle light,
and the rush of incense seeping
from hedges of sea roses, sherbet-
pink, consecrates the air or the
makings of this day when heaven
seems closest to us and would
willingly lift, fold and cast all
burdens seaward, leaving for us
this shoreline's indelible shining,
the benediction of milk-blue water and
tinseled filaments of whispering light.

Inversion

For Sharon and Michael

Brilliant as the day, the harbor could be
a second sky, a cistern of unblemished
blue, with tides beaten smooth by wind.
Past the deep grass of the inlet, a light-
house in exile, adorned in a pastoral
frock of arctic white, presides over the
long altar of tumbled stone while a few
gulls circle lazily above, like wisps of
incense rising high into summer air.
I am reminded, too, how the sky at dusk
seemed to take on the look of land –
say, an orchard just come into bloom
with stars, palest rose and gold glistening,
set adrift like tiny blossoms upon the wind.

Aegean Pools

The last of the receding tides
settles like glaze in deep crevices
of coral, leaving cauldrons of porous
rock with a radiant blue so pure,
so lavish, so filled with afternoon
sky, I'd readily bypass the mouth's
cold chalice and narrow candle of throat
and inject it whole. To hurry the feel,
without faltering, of dazzling azure
as it diffuses like an accelerant inside
the body, bubbling spume, expelling
a life's worth of afflictions. Besotted,
I'd hear the saline course across
the ancient aqueducts of the heart
and between the rungs of my ribs,
spooling through misshapen threads
of sinew, traversing trenches of
marrow, then towering up and into
the ruffled blossom of brain.
Jeweled flesh – fully infused –
and soul embrace the purge and
sweet corruption of bone and body.
And I see that I've become an
inflamed, blue-bright ghost,
unshelled and in damaged glory,
able to taste, at last, this beckoning,
bountiful and alien world.

Away from Water

Wanting for the flop of tides
or the guttural cries
of black-back gulls –

decibels beyond the fountain's
patter and listless rain.
Here, ears can't bother

to work for sound.
All is latticed shade, rounding
to languor.

Colors scatter then reappear
in brief intervals. Little to fear
or love

in this curated silence –
something far less
whole than the fervor

of ocean;
there, calm is motion,
the deft erosion of shores

by delirious waves.
Surely her garden wants
for this or something more:

the thrum and sensual wash
of tides, silt's bronzed varnish
and arcade-bright allure.

Now, as day's softly drawing
down, ornamental grasses flow
like gowns across an ocean floor.

Seascape

Muslin sails are lowered like burial
shrouds into the deep hollow of boats.
The shuffle of wind is a breath neither
taken in nor given out, and the water's
a seraphic-blue that's born from sky.

Just now noticing how easily sunlight
slips from one wave onto another,
as if it were in constant need to re-glaze
the water, and how the sandbar guides

the tides across long necks of sea grass
into calmer channels, leaving florets of
foam scattered upon the shore, as gulls
hover and drift in loop-back flight like
disciples in need of wind or direction.

Moonlight

Moon's a farrier affixing
shoes to the underside of
leaves, steel-bright, twirling
on shafts, fastened by wind.
some steal away running
barefoot towards gardens
and those that remain turn
and glisten, horse-shake
in mid-air, as if they were
unharnessed and about to
traverse and nick the upper
boughs on their way towards
heaven. Shadows cover the
lower branches like fore-
locks; stone walls and
fields appear littered with
discarded bridles and tack,
most half-hidden by waves
of uncombed grass flowing
past the tilted teeth of fence-
posts towards lower ground
where they flicker before
their silent pour into an
open wound of water.

Promises

Go, then, and gather
up your promises
as plentiful as queleas
rising near dusk or
the air-borne shoal
of pollen so dense
you could be looking
down upon the surface
of wind-wrinkled water.
Go in the dew-dripping
grass with your head
bowed in contrition
like a fiddlehead fern,
lanky arms dragging
an over-worn pouch,
bare feet shuffling
thru a shame you cannot
shake, and tell me
what it is you come
away with beyond
strands of spider silk,
naked needs and
a wayward whistle.

Autunno

Leaves succumb in sad splendor
to a brush of wind and are eased
to air in peaceful passage the way
gondoliers might nimbly push their
skiffs away from berths into wide
canals of calm water, watching
each one drift lonesome on blue
currents we cannot feel or hear,
while others, fledglings dawdling
on lower branches, seem to extend
a forefoot before the abrupt lift
and wheel back to branch as if
they've had a sudden change
of heart and so turn upon them-
selves, wingless, only to tumble
in free-fall towards earth in
tarnished light and settle near
battered brown husks, ankle-
high with brittle undersides
bleached by frost, until some
wayward gust raises them like
resurrected spirits that have been
touched and startled back to life.

Itinerants

Egrets are perched upon the barren boughs
like dollops of plaster, serpent necks rising
in the form of question marks or looping
low towards their long-tapered tails, soft
as candle wax, wreathed by water. It's
a transient world of shared impermanence,
withering and leaf-emptying, though
frosted, and the landscape's been
transformed into a luminous patch
of monochrome. A few months from
now, when weather hardens and the
marsh falls back to a matted and bitter
mixture of reeds, ice and brackish
water, I will return to an eerie after-
world where bare, cross-limbed boughs
are starkly pressed against a brooding
sky, boats are grounded and placed
belly-up near shore, and a widowed
silence induces reverie, and dream
of the bird's slow, laconic flight,
a heaven of manganese blue, and
winged seeds glistening like gold
dust in freefall towards some strange,
palpable communion with light.

In Late September

Near wakefulness beneath a grove of milk-
blue pines, needle-dripping boughs cuffed
by wind, the scent of balsam settling deep
within my lungs, while a crescent moon
severs the horizon, parting stars that are not
stars, their light's origin coming from somewhere
beyond these meandering valleys where
colors burn aloud and dusky foothills bend
back from the horizon, I weigh the tiny
pieces of ore or solder gleam I culled from
pools of quiet water and placed deep
inside my pockets where they will stay, like
tokens, to buy-back this day and whatever else
is left of a season that's slowly moving away from us.

Near Woodstock (VT)

Grateful for this day,
a slow-shuffling wind
and a sky of buttermilk
fringed with blue. Hillsides
ablaze in torchlight, blood-
orange bronzed, and snow-
dusted bales glistening in
a vacant field like wares
displayed on the sleeves
of a cutpurse. Frost fuels
the seepage into narrow
arteries of brooks so it
appears fragments of sun-
light, like ingots, are stored
there in lavish sheen, flecks
of gold disgorged down-
stream over moss-softened
stone. Birds seem transfixed
to boughs, like burls, while
leaves explode in updrafts
of air, muddling their ancient
flyways as they inch, year by
year, further up into these gold-
hammered hills to divide the
spoils of a season's passing.

Migration

And anyway, this is how the season comes
to voice, in the murmur of slanted light
and curious thrum of receding darkness,
all adjective and verb, expunging nouns
such that leaves become blurred, air-borne
lavish, and hills the low-lying flourish
of voluptuous purpling which is to say
let us dance around death and hunger
and loss with musings about how this
sad season, with its luminous, in-between
splendor and casual decay, outlives and
stands apart from a stark, guttural winter
while marveling at the silence of birds in
cooler winds seeking refuge in wingless flight.

Apparition

Disheveled autumn's deftly
side-stepped winter's grasp,
carrying in wide, blousy
pockets clouds of bees, brittle
nests and the easy currency of
pungent musk lifted from tea-
brown pools of leaf-rot and
acres of decay. He arrives poorly
attired in a worn, tweed cap
and thinning hair, mud-caked
shoes, frayed valise and a shawl of drab
scarlet woven from wool, blithely
traipses through the well-worn
paths of woodlands, dank ruts
of orchard and rain-glazed
pasture, and, bojangle-brazen,
turns windward and pivots
on his crooked walking stick
as he nimbly rises and entwines
with phantom light, pauses amid
the mottled luster of leaf-scatter,
drinks in the bright applause
of interloper crows, and then
bows meekly before sauntering
off into the upsweep of gray
gusts in his happy grief.

Autumn Birches

All sharply angled knees and gangly
elbows, serrated gold earrings candling

their slender napes of neck, they dawdle
like shy girls by the meadow's edge.

Well-coiffed with lacquered combs of
back-butter brick, their thin, contorted

wrists hold tangles of hair high above
their heads. In windfall, starved

secrets fall from their brittle tongues
and ribbons of bark, flailing

in October air, trick the ear and eye
into thinking they're lissome dancers

in pirouette. Yet, with morning
shadows in dim descent, it's easy

to discern that, for these gaunt curators
of splendor, any movement would be

considered an act of anguish.

Walk in October

It wasn't the bright bundles
of leaves that hung like paper
lanterns with stray tassels
of light or the vast poverty of
October skies, nor the fields
speckled with the stubble of
stalks, crumbling stone walls
and oddly shaped gourds that
looked like engorged rose
hips that had tumbled into
the dark culverts of a sodden
earth. Not even the flocks of
tongueless birds, rising and
falling, then reassembling
mid-air like gables, but the
fragrant, ill-begotten wind,
festooned with grains of straw-
dust, lambs-wool yellow, and
infused with the odor of varnish
and the dank rot of shallow
bogs and woodlands that's
holding me, deep-rooted, fast
to land, certain there's been
a lessening of distance between
this life and what's to follow.

Refuge

Dumbstruck by an autumn day draped
in a shawl of pale orange light, where
all the world appears dipped in lacquer
and apertures between the loose blush
of branches serve as stained-glass
windows that crease, then color, the air,
thickening with the fragrance of grapes,
wet hay and the tang of leaves in
slow decay. Where combs of meadow
grass are glazed with frost and sparkle
like beads of glass and the wind appears
littered with translucent wings, hay-
dust and clouds of thistledown, while
a chorus of migrant birds, falling
towards an open field where a patch
of snow's still bedded in shadow,
I await a season's easeful passage into
exile and into a cold, intractable dusk.

Near Uncas Point

Winter's coaxed this sandspit
from shore and outgoing tides,
in radiant disarray, have returned
land to the harbor by at least a half,
leaving mud flats adorned with
alluvial fans, hump-backed inlets
and high-stepping birds that seem
content to forage – with wings in
pockets – far from water. Trees
bereft of bark border the dusky
rubble of cottages sleeping in
disrepair, the throw of porch
lights leaking across lawns and
glazing loose planks of pier,
while ice wades out from snow-
dusted bramble into the scum
gleam of marsh, stretching farther
and farther from shore before
giving way to a confluence of
currents and the outflow of shale-
gray water. How very different
than a time when wrinkled heat
dazzled and hives of odor weighed
upon the air and each day seemed
an act of indulgence. Now, moored
in late October's amber, all of life's
been pared down from a glut of
rapture into something austere and
newly settled, frosted with salt spray
and tiny fragments of truant light.

A Day in Mid-October

The sudden silence
compels me to listen,
as if my older self is
whispering to slow my
steps and consider
this day's drowning in
a haze of amber and an
afternoon in search of
harvest – to see how
the leaves, like brightly
feathered birds, drift out
then up before faltering
downwards in slow exodus
with no way back to
their melodic nests.
Haystacks in warm huddle
house the incessant insect
hum that seems to stitch
brief pockets of silence
to pasture but mostly
the soft wash of wind
and the rich scents of
becoming or going as
time closes in on all
things even as burdens
are lifted, if only for
a moment, to find
their way back to
memory and dream.

Nuit Blanche

Late fall and near the edge of sleep
I take in, from behind a latticed
window, a courtyard covered with
the unclutched gold of fallen leaves
and the drift of steam entwined with
frosted lamp-light. The last grapes,
now odorless, darken in withering
skin, and dusk has descended like
fate beyond a fountain puddled
to stillness and into a riverbed
of oval stones that once carried,
in fluid splendor, schools of low-
lying clouds and leaf-bright boughs.
Loitering in day's damp aftermath,
swallows stumble from their nests,
as winter accelerates without scent
or sound, leaving sight alone to
extract something of meaning from
this brooding emptiness where all
light's nearly lost and the best one
can hope for is to become wedded
to wondering and dream of an early
nightfall brightened by snow.

Early November

Last leaf lifted and pitched to air
ample autumn quartered and done;
in the distance, entwined pairs
of birch are bowed
and broken.

A low sky settles eerily
and all light is spun
in down-shifting air;
a solitary crow
descends

to a death thrown clear
by snow melt running
downhill. Current veers
in leaf-thick flow,
upends

moss and matter.
All's now abandoned:
a bone, a muss of hair,
hope, and a tiny skull blued
with lichen.

Mid-November

A bedraggled day in mid-November
and a wave of fog fades and flares
in nickel-blue light, lifting past
branches of later-in-life leaves,
low stone walls and the muffled
pablum of an ice-glazed brook.
It comes to a kind of unmaking
over snow-dusted fields and
hollows, then appears to eerily
tilt and turn in a slow stratus curl,
as if coaxed into coupling
with the contours of earth,
embracing the come-hithering clutch
of late autumn.

Winter Birches

Here darkness gathers and spreads among
the glazed thickets and brittle-white splatter
of paper birches, slowly leaching out into
evening and far beyond the further wood.
Each disfigured tree quietly rises in angles,
bearing the grimace of crooked elders in
chronic pain, their anemic crowns, thinned
by cold, still bearing the promise of someday
reaching the floor of heaven, though their
fragile shoulders and limbs, bruised by
the icy malice of erratic, winter winds,
appear unable to heal, feathered bandages
of mottled bark flailing, as if they would
just as soon unchoose their burden of yearning,
wanting to simply buckle, fall and disperse
into pearl-gray plumes of nomadic snow.

II. FLORA E FAUNA (Flora and Fauna)

Great Blue

With morning's weight falling
away and a light fog lifting, I
caught sight of you, still as an
in-drawn breath, on the periphery
of a bay that was calm as pasture.
Gold-eye bright and tall as a child,
your sleek canal of neck funneled
a terrace of dusky blue into your
coin purse of body, eerily motionless,
as if you were in some nautical
stupor wondering how best to
navigate this middle stretch of life
or how to hold on to those things
that sometimes resurface only to
turn and fall away again, or perhaps
weighing how we might continue
to bear all that tethers us to earth –
at least until a wind swept you up
and led you, in tedious flight, across
tidal pools that smelled of salt hay
and the damp mantle of marsh,
early light sliding from your wings
as you became more phantom than bird,
a thing indistinguishable from the
tongues of tides or a cloudless patch of sky.

Cephalopod

Difficult to discern at first, but
the abscess of enflamed flesh
blossomed into a plume of color
that stood apart from the pink
crevice of coral, like a cloud
that's suddenly sun-washed
as it passes overhead towards
a farther horizon. Its haversack
head most resembled a gullet
or some strange moon that fell
from its axis and had its sphere
distended. Propelled towards
open water, weighted with three
hearts, it transformed into a sudden
flourish of howl, appendages adrift
in helix whorl, tortured tentacles
like free-flowing tongues or frayed
strands of rope unfurling and
contracting in sensuous undulation.
Shape-shifting its plush boil of body,
its blistered fingers balancing clusters
of oval nests, it easily achieves thrust
with a kind of unstudied elegance,
carrying it away in a backwash of
jeweled ripple from tidal appetites
towards some elusive pastures of
sea grass and porous stone. A forebear
of Scylla and gruesome leviathans,
its vulnerable, pebble-dashed form

now provides for little more than a
canard of watery ink blot – a lachrymal
of dark dew spilled from its bright
blue blood into a slip stream of water.

Hyacinths

Astounded by the wild plenty
of pink and purple splendor
pushing past soil, fragrant
arabesques rise up in intemperate
profusion and obliterate air,
emitting from eerily pursed
lips an enduring elixir I could
not prepare for like the intoxicating
flood of sweetness that some-
times comes from an aging grief,
slowly overwhelming the heart
and senses, leaving behind
the last earthly vestiges of some
unbidden grace or absolution.

Preservation

For Bonnie and Bob

Adrift in this calendar cold
l Iong for the breathy flute
of woodland thrush or the
hurried salutations from
warblers and wrens, but all
have taken to the astral fly-
ways known only to them.
Far harder now, in frozen air,
to crowd out these ear-splitting
emissaries from the underworld:
truant catbirds, tattooed jays
and crew-cut cardinals offering
up metallic hearsay for song.
Their audible convulsions call
to mind the jarring sounds of
dry thumbs trawled across a
window pane, a young child's
muffled cries moments before
sleep, or the hoarse whir of a
power drill. So much, then, for
the myth of new beginnings or
hurrying to hold the diminishing
sounds of summer in my head.

Peacock

Forsaking flight, trailing this lavish sprawl
of plume, bird's a spectacle of excess –
a luminous firmament floating near to
ground, a mardi gras of green that's falling
into an overbrimming muss
of Byzantine gold and sapphire blue.

Legs should buckle from the weight of it all,
yet colors cascade from the hair-pinned crest
through the tapered stalk of neck, swarm into
the jeweled body and ornamental tail
that's unfurled in iridescent drench, dressed
like a sorcerer's quilt some blunder of wind blew

up from ground. An opulent altar of artifice, the bird
prefers a wan and wasted earth to the fabled blue of higher air.

Spider Flower

Ephemeral pink queen,
petals dusting the tips
of stems as thin as filament.
Close to flight,

barely tethered, night-
blossoming, like flares spent,
dew dripped,
floating somewhere between

loam of earth and light,
as if touch meant
you might unwittingly slip
into a need

you'd rather lean
away from: drifting
into dusky retreat
and rudderless flight.

Just the way I mean
to stay adrift:
alone, quiescent,
like a skiff of ice.

False Brooding

Shoreline's a flop house in disarray,
littered with shells, bones and colored
cloth, the wrack line graced with
the rust stain of marine metals and
blossoming rot brought to surface
by the brew of ocean and incoming
tides. The caretakers reside just
above the beach-head, oversee this
collection of nautical bric-a-brac,
hurriedly leading waves towards
shore in a run-and-pause pursuit
of dreck the foam keeps offering.
In their tiny masks and priestly
collars, they're masters of artifice,
leading our eyes away, in feigned
affliction, from a small cavity of
gravel where blades of grass are
copper-colored and glazed with salt,
towards their olio's gleam and gore,
having left their nest unattended
in yet another form of hapless diversion.

Vultures

Welling up from ditches
like caretakers of loss,
they ride thermals
with large, lacerated wings
and long-stemmed fingers
delicate as coal dust,
relishing the idle drift
into black kettles of air,
traveling half asleep
for miles in search of
food, using only wind
for lift. Disciples of decay,
they nest with death
and indulge a life of
dark leisure, as meals
arrive without effort,
wind dispersing the
curious odors of carrion
and neglect from farther
fields, back roads or dumps.
Roosting in barren trees,
their naked heads appear
like enflamed gullets,
drowned in the colors
of garnet red or weather-
worn brick, stripped of
both feathers and flesh,
like the lives they carry,
weightless, up into alien air.

Mountain Laurel

Full dark an hour away
and above the water's edge
a fog thick enough
to walk upon. A ledge
tumbling into a trough
of gunmetal gray.

A sudden flash of pink stains
the air, and its brittle light
is soon extinguished.
Cruel unpetalings from a height
where gnarled branches perish
and blossoms remain

like stippled asterisks;
the dot and dash of sprays
perched upon thin, gangling limbs.
What else to make of this day?
The search for equilibrium
amid a season's detritus

leads to tasseled lamps
of dew-bright grass; wisps of fern
fallen and lifted stones,
lacquered logs, like urns,
holding lichen-crusted bones
that sing and glisten in the damp.

Bird's Nest

The crumble of hollow
that once held a clutch
of planets
with orbits drawn
into beds of feather down
and blossoms of pear,

an overwrought amphitheater
that once bled with sound.
Wind's begun
the soft silencing and let
water into the wattle's pouch
where shells imploded

into blue spackle.
I bend to touch
the long-ago tasks that
tied mud to ribbon
and twine lightly bound
to twigs and hair.

Little else to find there
in the brittle urn --
a quaint habitation
of the near-nascent,
songs longing for lush
like pieces of a broken life.

Loon

Buoyant, black-winged burl,
crepuscular swan, phantasmal thrush,
fallen from conical spires of smoke.

From your charred canyon of throat
dusk's inconsolable howl and thrust,
anguish made audible in spectral curl.

Channeling wail of wolf and owl,
a haunting dirge in whorled conch.
Shapeshifter, ember-eyed cinder, black-green

glistening, draped in iridescent sheen,
white lines flaking from speckled collar
into a tidewater of opulent swirl.

Your raw, unvarnished lament ushers
in so much more than darkness,
sets loose the very weight of living

into twilight air, guttural pain giving
form and texture to a sadness
that's other-worldly and moon-brushed.

Wild Privet

Your frayed
foliage has gone
lovely and turns
towards us in
milky sweetness
as your engorged lungs
exhale an outpouring
of pungent leach
dense enough to
displace air and
rivet footfall.
And even when
night drifts down
to porch light
and the orphan
moon floats up and
over you, leaving
scatterings of
silver gilt upon
your extravagant
tangle, the vast
flood of your
perfume swaddles
our empty hearts
and severs them
from the dark
spaces that
stretch between
stars and our
dreams of
wingless flight.

Vespers

Dusk's rising moonward from
a low nest of hills, unfurling its
mottled plumage and scattering
stars in holy hush. With day now
darkening and clouds squandering
the last of sun, the feldspar pink
and purple-blue smolder calls to
mind the small bird with a name
more mellifluous than its song –
Violaceous Euphonia – a finch
given to crackling trills and
sprinkled chatter, besuited
with tropic smear and sheen,
bearing bright strands of moon-
light upon its beak. Appears as
if it was dipped in a pool of indigo
except for those underparts of
dull enamel where its creator's
fingers cupped and bound its
tiny body in a rim of lunar light.
Perhaps it too hastily exchanged
song for the allure of dulcimer-
bright shimmer – unlike our drab
wood thrush, all earthy, river-
bank brown, whose liquid-slow
melody appears just before night-
fall, and lodges deep within our
hearts like a sweet grief or the
healing of no particular pain.

Green Turtle

Bearing this burden of a heart-shaped shell, I
spend my days drifting in the tidal sway of
shallow seas searching for underwater meadows
of lush sea grass, going hours without air
and months, if need be, without food; sleeping
upon the back of cypress-green tides or wedging
myself into cavities of coral, resting my sock-
puppet head before I ever return to my native
shore and once again lift this dense shell of
rippled varnish, the brown of sandal-wood
or broad-leaf tobacco, and an under-belly
that still bears the flakes of yellow moon-dust
that I swallowed when first finding my way past
the shoreline into deeper sanctuaries of water.

Colibri

As if a petal took wing
and was held motionless
amid a fierce crush
of light – a too sudden
sheen of flickering red that
challenges us to discern
feather from air, its song
from a hum of silence.

All a wayward happenstance:
air transformed to muslin,
a tiny tapestry turned
and finely wrought. Tail fans flat –
pulsating, tinsel thin –
jerks to vertical in a rush
of wind before the resurgence
to a raw and rhythmic chafing.

A miracle so small a thing
is constant motion, forsakes rest –
bird becomes inky blush,
emerges dusk-resplendent,
all color from form detached.
No less diminished, this apparition
burns to mid-air wet, dissolves again
into a smattering of freckled dust.

Sycamores

On summer nights, I remember
watching them sway in leafy
tangle, like young women
standing beyond straw-gold
parishes of pasture. Their
long arms extended in casual
scatter towards heaven, drawing
down the last of dusk across their
limbs like loose nightshirts, and
the palms of large, hapless leaves
whorled together in a quivering
rush of wind, and how the taller
ones seemed to be lit from within
and wear the stars like ornate necklaces
or bejeweled crowns while others
held the moonlight to their wrists
until morning stammered to window,
giving way to elegiac voices
as the mar and gnash of the everyday
set upon their limbs in blighted mottle.

White Tail

I've come unbidden to where pasture
stumbles over an outcropping of low-
lying stones and falls into mists that
drift in and out of woodlands and
deeper pockets of undergrowth and
am taken by the lack of fear in her
grazing, eyes near slumber and a
loose garland of grasses dripping
from her mouth, as if she knows
that I, yet another of the bipedal tribe,
am but a stray that life has softened
and parted from pain, senses dulled
by comfort, unfamiliar with the
perpetual pangs of leaf-dappled fear
where she waits upon fate and a twig
snap could mean the difference between
the near or far side of death. Nor,
until today, have I taken in such a silent
spectacle of flight, as she clears the
mottled stone wall with the ease of wind,
white tail lifted like a dismissive,
gloved hand, slipping as softly as prayer
thru the pleated curtains of leaves.

Cormorant

For a time, it seemed
the silence was forged
in fog, compressing the
tides as if a block of wax
had been warmed
and spread out
to the horizon,
or at least as far as
that dark drift of
sludge, a cormorant
exploiting currents
in sleepy drift,
soundlessly slipping
below the waterline
like a grief or burden
accustomed to
voiceless vanishings.
It's a well-perfected
dodge, smooth as
artifice, leaving but
a dimpling in black
dissolve. The silken
folds open and roll
back to calm while it
pursues silver-blue
shoals in watery
light, later rising
in phantom ripple
as a second, lethal
self, yards from

where our eyes
had expected before
the gibbering bolt,
the abrupt, ungainly
wing flap uncrumpling
just above water and
the fumble into flight.

Harboring Hyacinths

Fist-thick cobs could well
collapse under the weight
of their fragrant muscle:
curdled pink and purple
pestles that split the tender
lip of bulbs, and, in one
thrust, choke, swallow,
and sweeten air, and now
embolden, become near-
perennial squatters by the
bay window, make day-long
appeal to smell
with a raw, unremitting
redolence as if they knew
the sense most easily seduced
and addicted to their presence
and thus excuse their sins of
excess and untimely hope;
would have us believe,
in our winter-worn hearts,
that the next miracle is
manifest in the full flair
and gone-to-gold vellum
of morning lilies.

Egret

A sun so bright it seems
to burn blue from air,
while here, by tidal waters,
a vivid plume of cloud-
melt, a buoy's body,
legs as thin as the
shafts of a compass
and a face that's fused
with the sensuous neck.
The head now appears
too far ahead of its body
as it leans to surface,
patient as a muse,
hunched until instinct
compels the quick,
lyrical thrust of bill,
like a piston fired,
whistling thru the water's
canopy of olive-
green bladder-wrack,
neon shimmer
extinguished in
single swallow.
And the lethal
gaze soon returns
to water, much
the way memory
might pause in
pursuit of color,
touch or voice.

Oriole

Out towards the lower fields in early morning
light, mist hovers over the land like a medieval
shroud, and the hardened, wheel-worn tracks
take me past porcelain berry, wild radish and
an orchard long abandoned to chest-high grasses,
sumac and jewelweed. The fatigued arms of
apple trees are bent, swaddling shriveled fruit,
calling to mind the burdens that can buckle
and pull down a life, when wind shuffles the
shoulders of the tree-line and a sudden, bright
gash of day-lily orange – a cinder flushed
to flame – is set adrift in autumn air. The
beautiful body of bird offers a psalm of
fluid lament, a mellifluous, near-whistle
exquisitely delivered like an intercession
deserving of both earth's and heaven's ear,
seeking solace within this forgotten plot
of land on such a day when life remains
half-hidden and groans forth, and I,
with a heart contracted, look beyond the
bird to give thanks for such small splendors
in a world so badly broken where hope, long
ransomed, returns to us in the form of a wind-
borne ember and the simpler miracle of song.

Sweetgale

A buoyant whirl of catkins
and glossy leaf, thick as
language, seeking to sweeten
the sharp tang of decay and
salted air, but even you, bog
myrtle, cannot decide if you're
a creature of air, earth or water;
your tangled hamlet seems to
drift just above the water-line,
serving as a bulwark – a blue-
green plume that's near-enameling –
and holds onto this strip of land
and your feral necklace of shells,
bones, paper and glass, at least until
the advancing swell of tides loosens
your muddy belt, amputates the
luminous clay, and you become a lush,
lopsided bounty for water after all.

Horseshoe Crab

Assembled from happenstance and
horror, you'll find them, like discarded
hubcaps slowly spinning in shallow
coastal waters. They share resemblance
to a Kabuto casque with a loose flap
of shell suitable for a neck guard or
a discus that once skirted the surface
of water, came to rest and settled deep
into the mire and leaf mush of marsh-
beds where many have mistaken them
for flounders that have been fitted for war.
They could serve as a weed-whacker or
metronome, too, tail extending from
a sliced saucer of body, or else
an exclamation point that extends
the distance between surface water
and the arteries of salt-thick currents.
In another world, their long whip of tail
might be used as a stinger since they're
sisters to scorpions, armament of ten
jointed legs hinged to a vessel fit for
treading a sea floor in trundling unison
or spawning proverbs, like the one
that says in order to fend off extinction,
present yourself as something other than
your name and maintain a safe distance
from all manner of living things.

Common Tern

Most mornings I find you perched
upon the pedestrian bridge some
twenty feet above inlet water.
Tiny legs of safety-cone orange,
slender bill as bright as bittersweet,
with your black cap, you could
be a chickadee that's taken to salt
water, with a tail strangely split like
a divining rod. I wonder at the
sublimity of your style, though,
and the effortless lift up into air
and the coiled cradle into a small
fist of fleece, hovering as if you've
reconsidered the perils of waves
and windfall. Then the abrupt,
breathless dive and the rippled
plunder before the toilsome rise
to your perch for a brief respite
where I hear your guttural yawn
and note how quickly your narrow eyes,
freed of salt, return to the business of water.

Peonies

Floating above salvia's purple spires
of candle dust, these clutched fists
shadowbox with wind, juking
between sun and shadow, until
the leathery flesh blisters and
erupts into a fountain of fragrance
and garish extravagance,
ecclesiastical-white blossoms as
large as marble busts declaring
their intent to be of – and in –
this world well beyond a single
season, just the way an act of mercy
might emerge from a hard kernel
of despair to ease or mend a life.

Lodge with Pond

From a distance it appeared
like a hive salvaged and ferried
by snowmelt and wedged against
the far side of pond, pooling
light and swallowing sound.
But this malformed mound
of wattle and daub was built
by architects enamored of whimsy,
trudging boughs and trunks
of poplar and birch across
the wide lap of water, setting
them every which way into
that hollow and heavy knoll
where they return at nightfall,
nestled in the deeper quiet of
their drowsy den, comforted in
the knowing they have emptied
heaven of color and pitched the
landscape into a flat expanse of sky.

Peregrine

You have forged a habitat from our own,
reclaiming deformed spaces carved
into air: canyon walls of steel and concrete
and clouds drifting past in blue panels of glass.
All captured in the cold precision of your eyes,
round and dark as rifle barrels, straddling
a lethal beak and talons of caution-yellow.
Everything about you shouts *assassin*, and so
the Egyptians fittingly named a deity after
you – Horus, god of vengeance – with
gold flesh and plumage of flint blue and
graywacke. And now, wandering falcon,
urban sentinel, I watch you scale heights
in terrible torque becoming little more than
a pinprick, awaiting the hunting stoop when
you become an instrument of carnage folding
back a tail as large as your body, and wings
tucked, using tears to shield divining eyes
from wind shear. Tercel diving in dominion
like a trident blistering air and consuming
space faster than sound to where death itself
is dazed and abducted in a theater of raw conquest.

Sloths

Arboreal Atlas, aerial
acrobat of the languid
adagio, your elflocks
bleed thru fur and make
you appear like a throw rug
gliding in gridlock. You
have long abandoned a
want for land, and are
now a sedate sentry of
the understory, lumbering
through branches patient
as death, and traversing
air with a glacial grace,
where you eat, sleep and
even give birth, using a
fierce clutch of fingers –
tined garden trowels –
and lanky arms that
appear twice as long
as your legs to hoist
your earthly bounty of
body up and away from
ground. You mimic a
hammock mostly, limbs
adapted to an inverted world
and a life of suspension,
hanging like a fibrous fruit,
fur and face of a banded
coconut, with ears too
small for even sound to
enter, though your heart,

in its slow mercy, knows
there is little more to
survival than silence
and keeping to a height
that's nearest to heaven.

Swallows

Easy to envy
their erratic
exuberance
ascending with
scythe-like wings
in fevered flight,
rounding rooftops
and the crowns
of trees before
returning like
blind oracles
with a divine
purpose and
grim prophecies
to share. Their
delirious arrivals
and farewells
blend then blur
into fleur-de-lis
pivots and pirouettes,
chevron tails split
apart like lengthy
shears slicing through
charmed circles of
air, moments before
their tiny throats
of glossy indigo
morph into embers
as daylight falls

upon the tongues
of tides just catching
the last wink of sun.

Buckeye Tree

You've done quite well, child of chestnut,
so far north of your range, balancing
gaudy, crimson cupolas in mid-air.
Here, where tidal gardens harbor cloud-
banks of viburnum, I had not seen the likes
of you before and was startled by your
fiesta-bright flowers – arboreal displays
of arson – and have since come to learn
of your other name, *Firecracker Plant*,
well-suited, in my view, since you keep
your tinder-box fingers well-polished
for the balance of the month, and even
your smoldering fuses of stems will flare
in vulgar veins of color in the coming fall.

Starlings

Dispatched from dusk, an iridescent stubble
breaks over everything and lacquers the lawn,
and each inch of terrain becomes a mangle
of brunette sheen. Sodden acres are now
blanketed beneath a chattering with numbers
too vast for counting. In precipitous precision,
they rise, like a headwind suddenly made
visible, quickly extinguishing any creases
of light as each bird binds itself to the whole,
keeping tightly to form as if something
foreign and intent on anarchy might displace
it and lead the murmuration astray, none
daring to pull away from their dark destiny
and fretful portage between earth and heaven.

III. CASA E CUORE (Home and Heart)

Angling

Seeking nothing more than a patch
of shade and the calm expanse of
shallows, I've once again given
up on myself and struck at the
shimmer of light that rides atop
each low-slung wave – a delicate
dapping cast on monofilament
by easterlies towards this secluded
shore and I know enough about
fate to see that this day will surely be
one when only desperate souls
are caught and then mercifully
released after summer's gaff,
pewter-weighted, has lifted
me from my haunches towards a
benign heaven or at least that's
how the dream begins before
evening's emptiness when the
moon, in measured ascent,
maneuvers away from the
horizon and wades out into
the braided channels of sky,
using wisps of clouds as leaders,
while casting the luminous scatter
of more distant and nearer stars.

After the Death of a Friend

Because I've grown weary of blue
and want nothing more than a soundless
space to hide and heal, I choose this
darker hour of dusk and late-in-autumn
air. The foreboding, slow-moving clouds
of lurid violet and indigo ease into
evening while the season's last leaves
tilt and drip finespun streams of fleece
onto long tufts of grass. And I see how
yet another day's ending before it's begun
with too much loss, and how easily we
collect and coddle despair, and how
the senses, too, like the many memories
of you I sought to preserve, become
diminished things and this hobbled
muscle of heart would just as soon
utter its final farewell and leave this
world, following the moon's round
rind in slow transit upon a drowsy
wind with its unsettling truths of
fertile decay, colder days without
purpose, and the still-becoming darkness.

Woodwinds

They make the most of the raw
poverty of our breath, taking
leave from the blighted canyons
of our lungs and, in haunting
timbre, give eloquent voice to
anguish. Barely able to hide
their sadness, they make visible
the holes in our hearts, our bent
towards darkness and the beautiful
blemish of afflictions that often
come upon us like a sudden
abundance of dusk rising through
a narrow embouchure or the
moist lip of a wooden reed.

Another Life

For Father

The burden of a long life lifted, you
ascended from the dust of the dead
and the slow-shuffled elegies of the
elders, parting ways with memory
and the newly familiar, though
some things still held and anchored
you here: the whiptail of scar where
they cracked open your chest; quill-
white bandages that loosely clung to
translucent flesh; a deeply rooted
and tender-hearted grief; and coiled
fingers locked as if you were still
weighing how best to traverse the vast
abyss between this and some other life.

Song

Last night, I fell to dream
of Castle Combe,

its shambling mists and tawny stream,
the holy pathos of its homes.

Wind-washed clouds, the lunar gleam
of cream-colored stone.

And there, somewhere between
drowsy dusk and day, I stood alone

in fevered dream,
in Cotswold cold,

woke to air, moon-tide dimmed,
and the lulled hush of wool-

soft hymns
with all hope gone.

Near Positano

Shouldn't I have known,
reaching moonwards,
weak in the knees,
heart in free-fall,
that it would come down
to this?

Abandoned beneath a
bonfire of bougainvillea,
air scented with honey
and crushed almonds,
a golden hinge
of late afternoon light

closing just above
the cliff-face and the
torch-lit bay of heather-
blue water where, the day
before, beneath a brittle
ribbon of sunlight, you

wondered aloud about
the elusive bird's heart-
broken song and how
it seemed to be
giving away pieces
of itself or,

more likely, seeking
to weather a world

given to betraying those
of us who leap heart-
first before rising
in petal-fall.

As Yet, Undiagnosed

It fell, at first, soft as a scarf,
late arriving across the nape
of neck, only touch hurting
hard and then the sun-burst
shatter of perma-frost that lay
just below the thin mantle of
flesh, shoulder-blade quivering
and wingspan becoming
unstitched moments before
the sweet dissolution in what
felt like snowmelt filled with
slivers of broken glass, cascading
granules of anguish sliding
towards the breast-bone and
an empty reservoir of chest.

Befitting Blue

such as the pale
solvent leaking
from the periphery
of sky or the brightly
jeweled jay
flushed to wires
drooping like jowls
between utility poles
or the glass insulators
set atop the crossbars
like translucent
chalices of ice.
Perhaps the sneeze
of cornflowers stirring
in weedy plush or the
sham enamel spilling
from the bucket of
morning mussels
warming a pair of
damselflies – winged
bobby pins – locked
in contorted wheel
the color and shape
of the ring you
returned in your final
act of mercy last night.

Woodlake

For Father

Those final days spent
thirsting for air with an
anguish that made the
silence between each
gasp a moment of grace;
stale air tinged with the
medicinal smell of witch-
hazel and wintergreen; and
companions, still as clay
pots, overdressed and
tucked in corners, waiting
for the next gust of wind
to bear them away, while
you maintained your sad
confession and asked the
angels to be mindful and
to look over each of them,
and I watched you quietly
return between breaths to
the comfort of rooms that
you kept well-tended behind
lightless, hazel eyes.

Detachment

Because things often come in threes,
I await the conclusion to this trilogy
where items are accumulated by the
act of subtraction and there's a certain
enchantment found in moments of desperation,
like the time a plane, slipping into unhurried
descent, expelled a wheel that rolled, bodiless
and at a blistering speed, down the runway;
or the time, years later, when a compact car,
exiting the turnpike near dusk, ambushed
my windshield with a fountain of aspen-
orange dazzle, the rear tire having lurched
from the axle and fled like a convict, hurdling
knee-high guard-rails into the underbrush.
And so I await the third and final flourish
that's taking shape in my mind – where
fear's softened and I'm approaching the
periphery of some other world upon an
exquisite chariot that's veered off course,
with only one wheel, having reached the
right true end of a journey with too
little recovered and too much lost.

Chalk

For Marianne

Beneath the rusted red sheen of
frosted leaves, a sidewalk's
buckling and skittled by chalk
when memory knocks and I
think of you and those brute
batons of color, thick as ladder
rungs, and the ease with which
clouds, waterfalls and whirlpools
found their way onto a concrete
canvas. But mostly I recall the
bright blue door you said a person
could open if only they were kind
and pushed hard enough and how
the delicate furrows of pastel-
colored birds managed to pass
thru that same narrow doorway
since you were apt to leave it ajar
and how it could sometimes lead
those, who were young enough
to wonder, into a luminous space
where life could be brushed
away or simply colored over.

Effects

For Mother

Returning to the room where
you pretended to live aloud in
sallow light with the console
radio and its ornate filigree of
thread-leaf bronze, where all
sounds were familiar and
convincing to ear: sheets of
aluminum shaken for thunder;
cellophane crinkled to mimic fire;
bundles of books falling in place
of bodies; even corn-starch to
conjure feet tripping across snow.
But it was the uninvited grief that
proved too painful for voice
and came in the form of a young
life lost and memories stored
somewhere nearer the periphery
of heaven, looked after by the
patron saint of hopeless causes
who, you knew, would heed
your petitions since hearing
was the last faculty to fail.

Homestead

Ghostly birds drifting lazily to air,
like a fragrance that's been
eased from earth and holds near
to this day's downfallen heaven.

A few, solitary clouds appear
in sun-silvered drift, blend
into a smoke-like feathering
that wreathes the horizon.

The house, too, seems prepared
to drift and I also sense
it's loose, untethered stairs
would rise and extend

up into this basin of rare,
pearl-blue sky where they'd bend,
bearing the all of it, towards the nearer
stars aglint, arcing in perilous ascent.

Soapstone

For Sister Mary

I considered it a thing of beauty at the time,
a tiny tympanum that could have fallen
from an ancient pediment, its mottled surface
of wheat-yellow paling to olive-green, a florid
composition engraved with ornate carvings
of amphoras and urns, delicate as parchment;
fluted nooks evoking whimsy; and a sense of
motion with leaves forever frozen in wind-drift.
After years adorning bookshelves, it was placed
inside a tattered box, below the shifting strata
of sepia-washed photographs and candied dust.
Now, decades from her passing, the light she
brings through these wide, western windows is
well-timed, and helps to diminish this desolate world
of ice and wingless snow, the tangled motifs created
by long-withered vines on our trellis glistening
in a type of fractured glaze and so, too, all other signs
of the world's tenderness or feeble attempts at life.

The Sisters

For Greta and Ray

And so please be merciful unto them,
greeting with grace each spirit
arriving well-preened in lavender calm
and draped in a quarrel of white and black.

They may come humbled, seeking amends,
round rosaries clutched in their embrace,
like a child's puddled cheek or gangly arm,
wine-worn beads brightened with shellac's

crackled glaze. By all means, extend,
with the inexact delicacy by which we traced
the alphabet or the intricate forms
of angels clinging like silk to our backs,

forbearance. And hospice patience when
they curtly speak of disobedience and retrace
their deft use of rulers, pointers, backsides of hands,
but spare entirely those compassionate few lacking

bridal-white habits pressed and hemmed
to the wafered crispness of a eucharist.

Il Poeta

I'm dying empty,
having climbed past
middle age and now,
in this sun-latticed
space, where hope
and language end,
memory enters and
I try to reconcile all
that's passed with
what little remains,
weighing how I might
yet remake this life
of bad beginnings into
something worthy
of remembering. But
math becomes even
more daunting as we
age and it seems so
much more has been
subtracted, like the
way a winter's silence
within a balsam-blue
wood steadily and
irretrievably deepens
such that sounds become
something rare and
unsettling, like the
voice inside my mis-

shapened heart, even
as days shorten and
descend, as they must,
towards a cold and
certain darkness.

The Peabody Museum (1965)

New Haven, CT

Finally come to that congested case
and the counterfeit specimens
pinned to air –
Wood Thrush and Meadow
Lark, the Scarlet and Blue-
Gray Tanager; pressed to view,
the hummingbirds encased
in gilded throats of flowers
Then enter another exposition:
fossils from the Cambrian Era.

Interest poorly feigned, work
clear to songbirds in glass,
silently withdraw
to a habitat of shadow
and flit to a space where
all is tree-born hues
and wood notes hushed by glass;
there I come to know
how to listen and hear again.

But I fail to fathom
how feathers stir in stagnant air
or why nests of Blue-
Winged Warblers are placed
so close to ground, the House Wren
awkwardly perched upon a shoe.
Note the unsettling eye of the Vireo;

the pale green eggs of the Siskin
and the oval, flat-flared
face of a Snowy Owl.

Noted, too, the raptors
and how they pilfer sky
and seek to blend
with sun into air,
dissolving in kestrel-blue.
And Kingfishers studying
how light bends and travels past
water; the soft architecture
of air and shadow.

Through time held dear,
the Buntings and Orioles;
then a patch of sky and coal
that burns through glass
to eyes that never knew
trees harbored orange-gold
or drowsy blue. Still wait to hear
their small, painted throats
displace the sad conjecture
of grackles and crows.

Whither Atlas?

Perhaps it was the want for solace or
certainty that brought me back to see
what was left of the abandoned building
that was slowly being swallowed by
dog-eared undergrowth, green creepers
and tendrils of ornate calligraphy sprawled
across the white walls of ripening decay.
The structure abutted a glum corridor of
interstate where a penitent titan once
knelt atop the roofline and hoisted a
ponderous earth slowly spinning thru dull,
dead air before he was sundered by a
hammer-claw of wind or perhaps had
simply seen too much of this world and,
disenchanted, boarded a ghost ship from
the harbor back to Olympus and the safe-
keeping of his many daughters. Years on,
a man mired in middle-age with little hope
in his heart, recalls the stern admonishments
of the sisters who, decades before, declared
that he was, in fact, our Everyman, bearing
with uncommon grace, and since before the
time of angels, the darker burden of sin. Yet,
I remember thinking, with eyes half asleep
behind my wooden desk, that he, too, would
eventually leave us, tossing this round world
like some counterfeit currency into the wilds of wind.

Saint Boniface

For Brothers and Sis

Sometimes at night, freed from penance,
I close my eyes and drift towards sleep
awaiting the slow spirals of stardust
and droplets of light that emerge from
darkness and coalesce above some
ornate, oriel window, inset with leaded
panes of carmine, alpine green
and chalice yellow. Colors settle,
then soon abandon glass and dissolve
beneath a gilded asp, blending with
air and into body now rising beyond
the plane of altar, the velvet nest of
tabernacle, and the furrowed pews
worn to the hue of brown harness
as I watch a younger self cradled
in prayer and sowed with sorrow
waiting on the brighter hope and
splendor of sun suffusing plumes
of incense and illuminating the
arched, stained-glass window
depicting a solitary lamb in a field
necklaced by a brook and a gnarled
tree twisting up towards heaven,
blue leaves dripping, sky still bearing
the sacred scars of falling stars.

For Anna

Years removed from when you
first entered my life and wanting
to somehow make things stop,
what I remember are the many
times your embrace served as a
source of comfort, fevered with
mercy and grace and a willingness
to give always without restraint,
and how, later on, I came to recognize
how much of you took hold in my
wife – the surprise being it remained
unalloyed and endless, and wanting
such tender bearing to live on, we
gave our only daughter your name.

Dear Denise

It hurts all the more knowing I never
meant for the hurt to stay, or sting, but
I'm near-certain that it did, and from
this vexed and ravaged abscess of heart
I wish I could reach back and offer up
something that might pass for salve,
having been witless enough to think
I could exile the past and that the spurs
of adolescence would have been worn
smooth by now, and yet I'm the one,
decades disquieted by a hurt that's
like a canyon still deepening, who's lost
and laboring over the one-too-many mishaps
that can befall a hapless and untidy life.

Afternoon at the Atheneum

Hartford, CT

Remembering those silent
Sundays when I could read
chapters between patrons,
and the slow glide from
my station into the far-
gone galleries, past the
sullen statuary tucked to
margin, to take in the flood-
lit angels by Caravaggio
and Fra Angelico; Renoir's
depiction of Monet
painting in his garden;
or the haunting landscapes
by Claude and Inness,
while gold-buttoned
guards in navy jackets
with indulgent eyes
turned back to dozing,
silent as Etruscans, and
thinking how it was they
came to know I often
asked myself which works
to plunder and hang at
home long after they
drifted down dusty
stairwells and the last
quarter sighed silver
in the museum store.

Travelogues at The Bushnell Memorial

Hartford, CT

Ample hours each Sunday spent within
the nap-time air of the mezzanine where
proper ladies in pastels and pearls would come
and be afforded single seats by flashlight – no
doting companion to read aloud beside their
dying ear or idle layabout to relish the snag
of sound and crisp shush of stockings rubbing
thighs. Dearest acquaintances politely joined in
the muffled applause of linen gloves as the
matinee began with a deeper-than-winter
turning down of lights, transporting them
towards long-intended destinations of torch-
lit archipelagos, parks or fjords or, perhaps,
a cosmopolitan capitol filled with courtyards
of noon-time light. Always the warm, forgiving
faces of people awaiting their arrival when
lavish curtains slumped and lights lifted and
they too would rise, heel for balance, and
bob their way towards the loge and outer
lobby to configure this week's calendar for
collations and cards. Others long ago drifted off
to sleep beneath the dim constellations dancing over-
head, elegantly weathering to a dusty gold and gray.

Birch Mountain

For My Children

Descending headlong from empty boughs
like a lanky child, ill-at-ease;
sunlight awkwardly alights

upon blue combs of grass roused by a slow
surge of wind; clutched fingers released
to cushion the blow, mid-flight.

Propped upon bruised shins and knees,
the astonished body abruptly rights
itself, expands to luster and takes in the field below –

hobbled orchards and stubble where a few crows
gather to assess the new balance of things;
a landscape's nudged into brittle brightness.

Flock and forsaken farm are now clearly exposed –
shoe-button-black scatter and the keepers of night.

For Bobby

In Memory of Robert S. Smith (1954-2008)

Having made a wrong turn
a few miles back, I find myself
among empty farms and haggard
fields when a song I had unremembered
calls you back from those rough-hewn
places you still inhabit and I try to once
again make sense of your passing and
your shorter share of life. And how,
even as the years piled up, torn and
broken between us, I still carried
in my heart our easy crimes of child-
hood and the beautiful betrayals that
we were committed to keeping, though
even then endings were to be found
everywhere, even before you left
for a further coast, and with eyes
grief opened, I dreamed of you,
spirit dissolved, burdened by illness
that hollowed out soul and bone,
and left but a soft upheaval of hands
like these plumes of dust rising
behind me that will follow me home.

At Daybreak

First light frosting the tree line, and I close the door
on the rest of the house and leave the need for sleep
to others. At such an hour, with dark still lingering,
the stars blown apart and a waning moon near vanishing,
I've become too well acquainted with the dark dialect
of slush and wallop from this stretch of shoreline, the
pensive coo of mourning doves, the distant slap and
rhythmic carry of a south-bound train, and even the
scuffling of a lone, metal bucket listlessly pushed
back and forth across loose gravel by a vagrant
wind. The fragrance of wild privet permeates the
path that dips with the contour of the earth and I,
too, quickly leap past the bittersweet fragrance,
awaiting the weightless lifting of my feet from
luminous clay and the climbing out of my body,
but this day provides for a hapless harvest and
amplifies the emptiness, shrinking to something
less than healing. Returning home to houses
huddled around the harbor, I can feel the earth's
leaning towards another season as I take in
the clattering of plates, the reassembling rasp of silver-
ware being gathered up or placed down, and the
pungency of coffee and fresh-baked bread marbled
with cinnamon – the simpler luxuries of everyday
life that can somehow make the heart whole again
if only these much-mended eyes could learn to listen.

Bird's Eye

I'm referring to the clusters
of constellations that leopard
certain planks of maple –
sensuous aureoles of palest
gold that you might see floating
like candles in windows near dusk.
Whorled turbulence embedded in
the loose splatter of caramelized
grain without the oval thumbprint
of burl. Peacock veneer for rifle-stock,
stringed instruments, canes, cues
and even humidors. Its murky
wombs often interwoven with
the rippled ruin of flame-maple,
arcing like the cursive fonds
that mottle the orbed shell of
a hazelnut. Yet its lush calligraphy
tells us how grandeur is but a
state of constant erosion and a
series of harsh diminishings,
since the wood's delirious,
otherworldly splutter; its lavish
sprawl and erratic excess of eyes;
and its feathered homage to plumes
of steam and pools of looping
water also serve to weaken
the integrity of the wood.

Valle de Mulini

Amalfi, Italia

The weight of the past is also
fashioned from a raw mixture
of shredded cloths and rags, the
color of dove-gray clouds and
day-old ash, warily lifted upon
a screen of wire mesh into air,
pulp pressed to substance on
felt and dried to a milky gauze
that soon takes the form of paper.
To those of you, dear ancestors,
who worked these mills and knew
full well the far greater weight
and ceaseless pummel of merciless
machines and wooden mallets
powered by redirected river water,
I offer here, in the filtered light
of the *spandituri,* this damp sheet
that now bears a simple watermark
from one who, please understand,
offers a poorer mixture of tears
and torment, knowing, too, how
hard it is to hold this parchment
towards the light without thinking
of the burdens you bore and how
inadequate the words will be
that I am now compelled to leave,
in muddled spill, with each of you.

For Linda

On a midsummer day such as this,
cypress-scented air unfolding blue
over blue and floating down a tree-
lined street through our doors and
open windows, rooms gilded by
sunlight and calm as a chapel,
I still remember being stunned
to silence by your state of grace,
having long been abandoned
by god and betrayed once again
by body, and easing out of life
in a manner that was no less
luminous than this day, and some
time after, when all hope was
gone and with a heart still in
hiding, I remember finding
refuge in the abandoned stillness
that settles between waves and
the intermittent shimmer of
land-locked light, and then
holding my breath when an
osprey suddenly appeared
and hovered over the harbor,
free of wingbeat, doubling
down on life with its unsparing,
head-long descent into surf
and yet never seeing it rise
again from the surface of water.

Splinter

Easy enough to blame
the summer storm that
blew apart the upper
rows of shakes, or the
sweet relief of wind
and updraft of cedar
that lifted me into
a second-story musing
for the long tooth
of wood that bit
hard and settled deep
within a knoll of
muscle. Difficult
to tease out, it was left
well-embedded by crude
and hasty excavation,
eventually forming a
blue-black puddle
not unlike the icy
glaze one might find
at the bottom of an
inkwell – my first
tattoo, a tiny rosette,
that I'll house for safe-
keeping and turn to
each time I bend to my
work and know, full-
stop, that this is a gift
from the world of

curves, crooks and
edges that I've fallen
hard against.

Vestige

For Carmine

Too far fallen into autumn with its
old-growth trees in full revolt,
setting the hillsides aflame, to offer
more than a backward glance at
summer and its horizons of brushed
nickel and drowsy forenoons of
pearlescent blue, forever folding
into the malleable rustle of full-
crowned trees. Now, a scorched
landscape seems constricted by
clouds the color of corn-shock,
tapering into wisps that point
towards a heaven I still haven't
forgiven. I am unsure how to tease
out this time of year from memory
the way the morning fog's muffled
birdsong, extinguished the sun and
intimates the certain cruelty of after-
noon rain. It's nearly a year-to-the-day
when you, the eldest of seven and
our surrogate father, unexpectedly
passed and even now no amount
of grace or time will lessen the anguish
and thinking how the random plenty
of this season is so unlike the spring
where the tiny buds of new-growth
pink and frosted claret punctuate
the ridge-line and the back-quarter

of pasture with windfalls of promise,
while here the past comes rushing
back in a maudlin torrent of loss,
washing all hope away and I know
that I've lost you all over again.

Prometheus

Oh body be
breaking,
breast
bearing
wings wrought
in bronze
burnish,
cradled in
feathered
whirl of pour.
Unbound,
unblemished,
bent
buckled
blown
breathlessly
and bare,
blazing thru
bottomless
basin of
blue in
free fall
wrangling the
sacred
sublimity of
blessed, star-cindered
light from
heaven.

Hemlock

For Joseph Paul

Mere months since its transformation
from jeweled drizzle into an edifice
of staghorn coral, the conifer's
been fully disrobed and hollowed
by adelgid and leans forlorn,
brittle-boned and long-fingered,
a sickly thing now left teetering
in a wedge of wind, but the
artisan birds have taken refuge
there and reclaimed it, eerily
festooning it with thin garlands
of tinsel and patches of paper
entwined with scraps of purple
wool, sheltering a pair of
chickadees – caretaker nuns
with tiny faces framed by a
headdress of sooty black –
tending their arboreal garden
amid the gaunt branches'
grisly threads, sharp as shears,
like the cancer that burrowed
deep into your body and found
sudden sustenance in the honey-
comb of marrow and the pink
canyons of lungs and so took all
nourishment for itself and left
you a fatigued and fractured

host, leaving me to wonder
what more I can offer beyond
haggard hope, idle prayers and
the gift of glimmer found within
a sudden gust of mid-summer wind.

Chagall's *Still Life with Flowers*

Adrift in an aftermath of blue
and rising from rest, all things
appear to die little by little,
downcast eyes opening as if
to say they had once partaken
of all that brightly burns
outside the window, and
watched the silver stone of
moon spin and dissolve into
halo. Even now, though, with
the weight of life lifted, they
appear as half-healed, ghostly
hostages to want, affrighted
inhabitants of faded flesh in
search of solace or perhaps the
pleasurable, curious confusion
of sounds and odors rising up
from blossoms slowly relinquishing
life; the thin drizzle and purple ruin
of petals falling to table; the
warm reek of over-ripe fruit
and the alluring song of the
ancestral bird they had attended
and followed back to earth.

The Boulevard Montmartre at Night

Camille Pissarro, 1897

Emerging from the otherness of
nightfall and nocturnal rains,
a forgotten blue drifts down from
heaven and dusks the near-horizon,
the casements and cornices of ghostly
buildings, lending a damp, delirious
radiance to the boulevard, though it
seems all light's grieving and each
streetlamp's a long-tapered candle
just set to flame. Black parasols,
lacquered by the last of rain dripping
from trees, thread past quaint lines
moored upon a street that's suffused
with the gemstone glitter and brass aureoles
of shop windows and the fluttering of lamp-
lit shadow. The eye cannot help but
drift into the canvas, noting this is
how we often come to slumber: in
a half-light that flares then courses
away from us as we settle upon a
coach that travels the soft, gray-blue hush
between the worlds of sleep and waking.

Elegia

Perplexed by this poor
pretense of a summer day
and the lurid opulence of
leaves that fall just beyond
your window like tiny sails
unfurled and back-lit by sun,
ghostly transparent, each
exquisite in its air-borne
decay, some ablaze in yew-
berry red or street-lamp orange
fringed with the blush of
misty green-gone-yellow,
I too find myself adrift with
little hope in my heart,
bartering with a grief that
memory had managed to
somehow tuck away in
darkness until sunlight
entered the room in latticed
scatter, and stifled sobs
became eerily still as you
cupped my hand with a
gesture as soft as sleep
and, in a diminished
voice, told me that, even
when giving ourselves
up to grief and pulling
away from the world,
hope will still find its

way back as time
staggers on, fumbling
faith and forgiveness.

Neon Pegasus

If only it were that easy to clear
the elevated canopy, pushing off
thin, knock-kneed legs, caught
somewhere between earth and air,
clearing oily pools of nickel-violet
and snow-drifts fringed with fragments
of frosted metal and broken glass;
petrol pumps standing like a pair
of cyclops – their milky eyes floating
above plated shoulders, watching
you in still panic and wondering how
it is you rise like an electric etching,
each staggered leap aligned with their
dumb pulse, to settle in some unchartered
constellation, only to sense the true depth
of darkness and return again and again
to savor the gift of ghostly wings or,
more likely, a much nearer emptiness.

Vertigo

Grateful for ninety-degree walls
strong enough to prop up a man
stumbling from his bed, using
panels of ship-lap for ballast,
I feel as if all of earth's listing,
bureaus and thickets of doors
betraying me.
Then heading into the hamlet
of hallway, where objects
confound and blur, I'm
soon grabbling forward like
a marsupial trying to keep
its head still, unsure of whether
God has granted me two legs
or four. I'm in an alien world
where light's distorted, the
final destination is unknown
and my time of arrival is
a bad guess at best. I may
yet rise, though, and become
an enfeebled Ptolemy,
able to posit the theorem
that we do, in fact,
sit at the center of chaos.

Evening in the ER

Knackered troupe of heartache, dust-
festooned carnival in a God-forsaken
land, where anguish comes full-throated
and all grace and giving have been called

back to heaven. Aptly, the drunken
badger, sucker-puncher clown assailed
by a bevy of cops like distraught birds
in pursuit of a trespasser of nest.

Or the young bride, rawly afraid, kissed
by amulet of crowbar, matrimonial
bouquet of day-old blood, wedged
beside twin widows, fortune-

tellers with flesh as bright as
metaphors, dry hearts crackling
like tumbleweed inside their
chests. Inconsolable satyr of

pathos, wailing polyphony, in
search of phantom sleep or the
nub of noose swinging up and away
from memory and sublime afflictions.

And me, hobo of acute vertigo, elegiac
epilogue, ossified dirge, trundled off
to some austere sanctuary for those
who seek nothing more than a way out.

Tiny Mercies

For Debra Ann

Like the way you caress
your cup of coffee and
cradle it near your chest
as if to warm the heart;
or your pathless
humming when tripping
through tasks; the
endearing way you
recoil from cold or
tuck loose strands
of hair inside your cap;
or the noble want to
always place the needs
of others before your own.
How different from
the aging misanthrope
who watches you, heron-
still, with eyes half-closed,
weighing this morning's
endearments that nibble
away at the dark spaces
where hunger hides
even as the heart expands.

Ociosidad

A day worth losing in the company of
Desmond and Getz, setting out a shallow
bowl of oranges while a diaphanous blue
flame purrs then nuzzles into the beat-
up belly of an antique kettle. Rain's punching
its way thru wind and collecting in streams
that traverse windows in strange geometry,
forming tiny pools laden with nascent light,
neither bright nor dark, but still somehow
glazing the quiet metal of the balcony with
its empty flower pots and broken broom.
The abrupt creak of floor boards as the
house stirs, settles and shows itself submerged
in the hushed shimmer of the vintage mirror,
freckled and de-silvered, with a cold hearth,
pocketfuls of to do's and dusty sorrows
and a want to learn from my mistakes, as
the drowsy fan whirls on in muffled drone,
unwinding the day like a clock, stretching
each tedious hour as thin as a day-old promise.

Swan of Tuonela

After Jean Sibelius

It's the plaintive score that first drifted into
my ear and onto a sandspit where it stayed,
like a conch, harboring sounds and releasing
them at times such as this when I am given to
remembering. Delivering me now to the time
of your departing, and asking what I would give
to have you whole and once again in safe keeping.
But death calls us into and not away from this world
where the cor-anglaise, haunting and unhurried,
speaks with a grief too deep for words, floating
above the shuddering strings in dusty sail, much
like the mystical swan upon the underworld's
lamp-lit waters, cold to the wrist, nibbling like fish that
fell into a young boy's pockets and swim with him still.

Teeterboard

Surely, you'd be the one
grafted to ground, mid-wife
to gravity, impervious to the
seduction of wanderlust,
preferring the comforts of
the companionable, the
divine intimacy of the
familiar and well-spun.
Blown upwards, I'd be the
impulsive diversion, up-
soaring wingless, unburdened,
seeking release and prone
to dawdling. Yet we're both
well acquainted with the gross
disparities in balance and
the rise and fall of moments
that dwindle, distract and yet
in some sad way still define a life;
and how, at a time for leveling,
you also reminded me how
time and distance can so unsettle
the world and how I'm the one
who's most afraid of heights.

Homebound

You should go now, while the children
are asleep and before the sky blues up.
Mind the fog and the parkway even at
this early hour as you head north and
time works backwards with each new
mile. No, love, it can't be helped and
it can't be undone, but perhaps we can
learn to love from a greater distance.
I'll remain, unplaced and dream-weary,
polish my pearl-handled revolver and
cradle cups of coffee with coarsened
hands, nurse wounds long past healing
and leave to late-departing birds our
last bags of flaked maize and thistle,
let the dog out and wonder if he might
join me in my petitions to Saint Jude,
maybe set the flame to brighten a lightless
room. And, I'll be certain to say goodbye
to our inventions that hobble down hallways
and tumble out into an unmowed lawn
while an early morning mist picks at the
flaking clapboard even as the shed begins
to disappear and the neighbor's tree,
gnarled branches bandaged in white gauze,
sighs in its appleness and a single fruit
falls in the damp dribble of autumn air.

With Affection, Athens

Before departing for good into
the ether, following an arc of sky
bent in such a way it compelled
all eyes to follow you, o goddess,
in tender upwards, you dutifully
extinguished the bronze cauldrons
and pallid candlesticks of squill,
washed your sanctuary and swept
the dust and ash from between the
fluted columns set atop that brute
plinth of stone, and watched the
decay descend and scatter, unperturbed,
in arid air across the isthmus and
settle between the vapor-soft leaves
of blue jacarandas and honey-combed
houses as stark as the land, where
votives rise from beneath the floor-
boards of scooters in bee-bright
whine or across the shag-bark of
frayed, overhead wires, or the scrawl
of graffiti left by deranged deities
who now dwell beneath the thread-
bare awnings of abandoned buildings
buttressed by slabs of concrete,
where the sharp scents of olives
and chestnuts, musky hay and over-
ripe vegetation, mingled with cypress,
leather and stagnant water, are offered
up to your ghostly legions and triremes
whose broad sails once burned as bright
as embers upon your haze of harbor.

Twilight, New Haven

How readily the soul delights in
the frosted glow of lamplight,
when all the world seems to pause –
perplexed perhaps – by a sudden
abundance of ornament as waves
of ruby-throated violet envelop
the sky, spreading above and beyond
the boughs, falling in delicate demise
not from but thru the clouds, befriending
air, unspooling like a bolt of silk that's
become embedded in trees and unfurls
into the brooding, communal dark
between buildings, carpeting courtyards
and dimming what appear to be candle-
lit windows, while the muffled peels
of church bells bleed out to echo and
hang in autumn air just a few hours shy
of frost long enough to console, lift
and nearly heal our hearts before the
settling of life back into the fetid musk
of yet another lost November evening.

Lethe

Half-awake sleeping,
I feel a lightness settle
over eyes and limbs,
chest lifting
as if in dream,

like the line between
despair and anguish.
Now I'm swimming
in pearl-gray water, metal-
bright. I'm thinking

I might yet go under.
Soon, I'm drifting,
and memory, from shore,
unwhispers me asleep
and I cannot wake.

Hollowed bones ache,
and a keel-deep
calm follows. Vapor-
soft eyes can hear lightning
without sound or wind or thunder.

To My Grandchildren

Gathering up this aging heart
that's loosened and fallen again,
unable to rise, leaving a space
inside me while watching you
sleep, hurtling aimlessly into
dream, after a day seaside
collecting shells and snails,
housing them in bright buckets
and counting each one like
wishes carried upon incoming
tides crusted with light and
then taking in, by firelight,
the day as it undresses and
puts on a night-time sky,
with story upon story told
or to be continued like your
blissful lives that I pray are
no less full and never-ending,
convinced that this earth may
well be our only heaven and
the best we can do is to try
and hold such days close for
safekeeping and keep loss at
bay, and so what I'm now
asking is to forgive those
of us who, deep in life's
winter, watch over you and
once again dream of being
young while hoping we've

bequeathed something of
worth you might hold onto
and never outgrow.

ABOUT THE AUTHOR

Twice a 2021 nominee for the Pushcart Prize, John Muro is a graduate of Trinity College, Wesleyan University and the University of Connecticut. His professional career has been dedicated to conservation and environmental stewardship. His poems have appeared in numerous literary journals and anthologies. His first book of poems, *In the Lilac Hour*, was published in the fall of 2020 by Antrim House. He currently resides in Guilford on the Connecticut shoreline with his wife, Debra Ann. You can contact John at jtm254@comcast.net or visit him on Instagram @johntmuro.

This book is set in Garamond Premier Pro, which had its genesis in 1988 when type-designer Robert Slimbach visited the Plantin-Moretus Museum in Antwerp, Belgium, to study its collection of Claude Garamond's metal punches and typefaces. During the fifteen hundreds, Garamond – a Parisian punch-cutter – produced a refined array of book types that combined an unprecedented degree of balance and elegance, for centuries standing as the pinnacle of beauty and practicality in type-founding. They were based on the handwriting of Angelo Vergecio, court librarian of the French king, Francis I. Slimbach has created a new interpretation based on Garamond's designs and on compatible italics cut by Robert Granjon, Garamond's contemporary.

Copies of this book can be ordered
from all bookstores including Amazon.

•

For more information on the work of John Muro
visit www.antrimhousebooks.com/authors.html.